HORSE
TAILS & TRAILS

HORSE
TAILS & TRAILS

A FUN AND INFORMATIVE COLLECTION OF EVERYTHING EQUINE

TEXT BY LISA DINES

WILLOW CREEK PRESS

© 2005 Willow Creek Press
Text by Lisa Dines
See page 119 for photo credits.
All cartoons © Leigh Rubin, and used by permission
of Leigh Rubin and Creators Syndicate, Inc.

Published by
Willow Creek Press
P.O. Box 147
Minocqua, Wisconsin 54548

Library of Congress Cataloging-in-Publication Data:

Dines, Lisa, 1955-
Horse tails & trails : a fun & informative collection of everything equine / text by Lisa Dines.
p. cm.
ISBN 1-59543-240-X (hardcover : alk. paper)
1. Horses. I. Title: Horse tails and trails. II. Title.
SF285.D584 2005
636.1-dc22

2005030106

Contents

The Horse's Story

Fifty-five million years ago in the Eocene epoch, a fox-sized animal with four toes on its front feet and three on its hind feet crept through the swamps and nibbled on plants in what is now Utah and Wyoming, and also in parts of Europe. This animal is now known as *Eohippus*, which means "dawn horse" in Latin, and it is the first ancestor of the modern horse.

Thirty-seven million years ago, when the forests thinned and grass became more abundant, the second ancestor to evolve towards the modern horse was *Mesohippus*, which was larger and swifter and had only three toes on its front feet. Seventeen million years ago, we know *Merychippus* was present in North America by the fossilized remains discovered in the Northwestern Great Plains regions. Up to thirty-five inches at the shoulder, these little horses lived in herds and had the same large, strong, grass-grinding molars that modern horses do. On its feet, one central toe had become larger and harder while the others had receded, giving it hooves.

Twelve million years ago, *Pliohippus* roamed Colorado, Nebraska, the Dakotas, and Canada, and migrated across the Bering land bridge and became prevalent on the Eastern hemisphere. *Pliohippus* has been found in North and South America, Asia, and Africa. Finally, in the last two million years, *Equus caballus*, or the Modern Horse, emerged as the beautiful animal we know today. The modern horse died out in North America, however, due to the Ice Age or predation by man. When the Spanish came to conquer and settle the Americas beginning in the 1500s, they brought the horse back to North America.

Mesohippus (above) was the second ancestor of the modern horse. It lived in the Oligocene period, 35 to 40 million years ago.

Twenty thousand years ago, primitive horses were drawn and painted on cave walls in France, where they were depicted as being hunted for food. Horses were not domesticated, however, until 4,000 to 3,000 BC. Horses were ridden and used to pull carts and chariots depending on the user. In the Middle East, wheeled vehicles were pulled by horses, while in mountainous country the horses were more often ridden.

By 1,500 BC, harnesses and breastcollars had replaced the yoke that was typically used on oxen, allowing the horses' shoulders to pull the load. Bits were first made of bone, horn, or wood; bits made of metal emerged around 1,200 BC. Antler cheekpieces attached to soft mouthpieces have been found at archeological sites north of the Black Sea, as have horse teeth unearthed with unmistakable wear from metal bits.

Chariot racing was included in the Olympic games in 680 BC (the 25th Olympiad). The Olympics were banned in 393 AD by the Christian Emperor of Rome. The modern Olympics were revived in 1896, and the first mounted events were held at the 1912 games.

As humans began to ride the horse, they used them to gain dominance on the battlefield. The Hittites in 1345 BC developed a detailed war horse training regime, while the mounted Scythian Cavalry successfully invaded other territories around 670 BC with archers riding on horseback. (It is believed that the Scythians also invented pants at this time because of horseback riding.) In the fifth century, Attila the Hun conquered his lands from horseback, and the Chinese, who invented the saddle and stirrups, had a powerful mounted light cavalry. Stirrups were first invented to aid in mounting; initially, only one was attached to the saddle, but by 322 AD, two stirrups were common for Chinese equestrians. Early Asian horsemen also made protective horse booties from leather and plant material for horse's feet.

"Man on Horse Back" petroglyph from the Sand Island Recreation Area near the San Juan River in southern Utah.

Around 400 BC, a Greek horseman and cavalry officer named Xenophon wrote a kind and sensible treatise on riding and caring for horses called *The Art of Horsemanship*, which is still read today. His advice about choosing a horse includes: "The neck should not be thrown out from the chest like a boar's, but, like a cock's, should rise straight up to the poll and be slim at the bend, while the head, though bony, should have but a small jaw. The neck would then protect the rider, and the eye see what lies before the feet. A horse thus shaped could do the least harm, even if he were very high-spirited; for it is not by arching the neck and head, but by stretching them out, that horses try their powers of violence."

The Romans were very fond of their horse-drawn chariot racing. Programs were sold, and each chariot team had its own color of racing "silks," personal breeders, drivers, and veterinarians. To get race results to people off-track, carrier pigeons were let loose with the news.

MYTHICAL HORSES

Benevolent and powerful, mythological horses and half-horse creatures abounded in ancient lore. The "hippocamp" was a horse with a serpent tail that pulled Poseidon, the Roman god of the sea, across the ocean. Poseidon was also believed to have created the horse. Helios, the God of the Sun, is pulled across the sky every day in a hold chariot drawn by winged horses. Folklore of both India and Denmark have similar tales of horses pulling the light of day across the sky. In Scandinavian mythology, Odin's eight-footed stallion named Sleipnir carried him over the sea, or into the land of the dead.

Pegasus was a Greek winged horse tamed by the Goddess Athena with a golden bridle; Pegasus carried Zeus' thunderbolts and the Goddess of the Dawn, Eos, on his back. In Greek mythology, the centaurs were a race of beings with a human upper body and an equine lower male body. The centaur Chiron was admired for his wisdom and proper conduct. Epona, the Goddess of Horses, was worshiped first by the Gauls and Celts, then the Romans.

A white horse symbolized purity and had tremendous value in Ancient Greece.

The earliest metal horseshoes were invented by the Romans and were known as "hipposandals." They were not nailed to the horse's feet, but tied on with leather thongs. The Roman road system stretched 50,000 miles from Syria to Britain, and horses were ridden and driven over them with great speed to deliver mail, goods, and travelers. Around 1000 AD, Europeans started nailing metal shoes on hooves to protect them against excessive wear, and this has remained the custom today.

DID YOU KNOW?

The U.S. Cavalry field-tested lightweight, flexible aluminum horseshoes in the 1890s, but determined them not to wear long enough for military service. The first U.S. patent for an iron horseshoe-manufacturing machine was issued to Henry Burden of Troy, NY, in 1861 which made up to sixty horseshoes an hour for the government.

The name farrier comes from the French verb *ferrier;* which means to shoe horses.

The sidesaddle was popularized in England by Anne of Bohemia in 1381 so that women could ride with their voluminous skirts comfortably and stylishly. This same European princess brought with her to England a carriage made in Kocs, Hungary, when she married Richard II. From the town of Kocs came the word "coach."

Ever since horses have been ridden, people have invented different forms of saddles to help ease the ride. Today's saddles are designed for specific kinds of riding: western, general use, dressage, and sporting. All saddles have trees that are the basic forms the saddles are built on; these come in different horse widths, and are made of either wood or synthetic materials. A breast collar to match the saddle is frequently used to prevent a saddle from slipping to the side.

"Y'all have got a lot of nerve complaining to me about being saddle sore."

Modern jousting reenactments like this one are popular today.

In the Middle Ages selective breeding brought about larger and stronger draft-type horses. The size of men who rode horses had also increased from the small Mongols, Huns, and Chinese to knights and kings like Charlemagne (Charles the Great) who lived from 742-814 AD and stood six feet four inches tall.

A knight's armor weighed up to seventy pounds and larger, stronger warhorses increased the impact of a knight's lance thrust. Warhorses were shod with nail heads protruding from metal shoes so they could trample and injure enemy foot soldiers. Bits with long shanks and high ports were also used on these warhorses, called "destriers," and spurs made of iron, brass, silver, or gold (depending on the wearers' status) were employed.

Medieval folk also rode smaller "palfreys" (shorter, long-bodied horses with comfortable ambling gaits) and "coursers," lean, hot-blooded horses built for speed. Jousting tournaments became a popular form of recreation to prepare knights for real battles.

Horses were first used for agriculture on a major scale in the Middle Ages. Today, you will often see hanging from the browband of a draft horse's bridle a decorative circular metal piece called a "horse brass." Originally from Medieval Europe, these were made of brass and hand-hewn in some circular shape to represent the sun, or the light, which was thought to ward off the devil, or the darkness. Later, when horse brasses were widely manufactured by machine in iron they were made in more complex detailed shapes such as the owner's trademark, favorite animals, or other pleasing designs.

Draft horses

The 1700s saw European colonists enter the budding United States in great droves, and along with them they brought their useful and beloved horses. The German Mennonites in the Conestoga River Valley of Pennsylvania invented the Conestoga Wagon in 1733. The wagons required a team of six big draft horses and were made of strong materials such as hickory spokes, oak frames, and poplar sideboards. The floor of the wagon was higher at the ends than at the middle so goods shifting during transport would fall to the center and not affect the balance. The linsey-woolsey cloth over the top was white, the wheels bright red, and the body deep blue. These red, white and blue "prairie schooners" pulled by large, strong horse teams transported pioneers across the Santa Fe and Oregon trails to the Pacific Coast, and contributed greatly to the nation's growth.

Wagons and buggies of all sorts, lone horseback riders, and pack horse strings of up to fourteen to fifteen horses, mules, or oxen carried goods over Indian trails of the early United States. Wooden platforms ferried horses across large rivers. Military roads between forts were constructed through virgin forests, and between towns John MacAdam introduced "macadam" roads paved with layers of packed gravel. The American frontier was thus opened up to public stagecoaches seating up to twelve people and pulled by a team of two to four draft horses. Light pleasure wagons pulled by one pair of horses took families to church on Sundays and, hitched to a wagon, drove goods to market the rest of the week. The one-horse "shay" (from the French word "chaise," meaning chair) had two wheels, a fixed top, and a body that hung on straps that acted as shock absorbers, and was a source of fast transportation that required only one "horsepower." In the 1700s, because of the ever-useful horse, it was said that "no one walked save a vagabond or a fool."

"Well, no wonder we're not getting anywhere! Can't you follow directions, numbskull?! ... Y'all went and put the cart *before* the horse!"

© Leigh Rubin

Laws passed by early Spanish conquerors prohibited any Native American Indian from riding horses, but after the Pueblo tribes in New Mexico ousted the Spanish in 1680, many Spanish horses were left behind that the Pueblo Indians tended, rode (and also ate), and began trading with neighboring tribes. All Native American tribes were quick to see the value of the horse, which they soon relied on for hunting, transportation, sports, and warfare. The Plains Indian tribes soon became the greatest horsemen and mounted buffalo hunters of the 1800s.

In the 1800s, American industry relied heavily and primarily on draft horses for transportation, manufacturing, and agriculture. Large, newly-invented farm equipment like the McCormick reaper necessitated increased size of draft animals to pull it, and thus more importation of heavy draft breeds from Europe. In 1867 the rural horse population in America was estimated at nearly eight million. The loss of a farmer's horse often meant his ruin, since he and his family depended on Old Dobbin for so many things. Horses hauled goods, pulled omnibuses, cabs and carriages, agricultural machinery, and employed a whole industry surrounding them consisting of carriage makers, wheelwrights, harness crafters, feed merchants, farriers, and stable keepers.

Shoeing a horse in 1842 cost 5 cents, or a load of corn.

DID YOU KNOW?

Paul Revere didn't own a horse. The patriotic silversmith had to borrow a mare to carry him on his famed midnight ride to warn the town of Lexington, Virginia, that the British were coming, and her name was Brown Beauty. "A very good horse" was Revere's description of the brave, speedy mare that successfully carried him past the first patrol of British soldiers on the trip, and into Lexington. But when a second patrol encountered Revere, they confiscated Brown Beauty to replace one of theirs that was tired, and Paul Revere had to return home on foot.

In 1860, the Pony Express delivered mail between St. Joseph, Missouri, to Sacramento, California—1,966 miles in ten days—relying on fresh horses every ten miles or so that were waiting at relay stations. In 1862, the telegraph and railroad replaced the Pony Express, but horses still had to deliver goods to "The Iron Horse." "Buffalo Bill" William F. Cody was a Western frontiersman and Pony Expressman who rode a record 322 miles in 24 hours and 40 minutes using 21 horses, mostly small "California Mustangs." Four hundred horses were purchased to stock the Pony Express route. Thoroughbreds, mustangs, pintos, and Morgans were most often used.

The United States' military history is full of generals and presidents who were fine horsemen. George Washington had a 16-hand chestnut Arabian stallion named Magnolia who he later traded for 5,000 acres of land in Kentucky. Washington had a genuine fondness for horses, and was an active participant in breeding, racing, dressage, and hunting. Several specific breeds were mentioned in Washington's stable records: Narragansett, Andalusian, Chincoteague Pony, and Arabian. He also owned several draft horses. Washington's personal favorite war horse was Nelson, who was given to him by Brigadier General Thomas Nelson.

General Robert E. Lee was always extremely careful to give close attention to the shoeing, girthing, nose-band, and the folding of the saddle blanket for his horses. Lee once spotted a soldier in Virginia riding a four-year-old grey. Lee started to refer to this young horse as "my colt," said he would need him later in the war, and finally bought the horse for $200. Lee named him Traveller, and sung the praises of his "short, high trot, and fast, springy walk," and his "endurance of toil, hunger, thirst, heat and cold, and the dangers and sufferings through which he passed." Traveller was eventually replaced by Lucy Long, "a low, quiet and manageable little sorrel mare" when General Lee got older and the grey's "nervousness, vim and vigor" caused an accident that broke both the General's hands. Both Traveller and Lucy Long outlived General Lee.

George Washington

Saddlebreds served as mounts for many famous generals: Lee rode Traveller, Grant rode Cincinnati, Sherman rode Lexington, and Stonewall Jackson's mount was Little Sorrell.

General Ulysses S. Grant went through a succession of mounts. He rode Fox, a roan, and Kangaroo, a Thoroughbred, on the battlefield although others thought they were too ugly to ride. His favorite horse was Cincinnati, a gift from a dying man, a 17 hand Thoroughbred and offspring of the famous Lexington, the fastest four-miler around. Cincinnati carried Grant successfully through many battles, and was offered $10,000 in gold for him, but Grant refused.

In 1876, at the Battle of Little Bighorn in Montana, the U.S. Mounted Seventh Cavalry under General Custer lost their leader, all 231 of his men, and all horses except one named Comanche, to the mighty allied forces of the Teton Sioux, Northern Cheyenne, and Arapaho. Found seriously injured but still alive on the battlefield, Comanche (reportedly of mustang lineage) was rescued and nursed back to health. There were other horses reported to have survived, but the Indians had no use for the injured Comanche and left him behind. Comanche was ordered never to be ridden again, and was kept at Fort Riley, Kansas, until he died. Comanche is now stuffed, and permanently displayed at the National History Museum at the University of Kansas. The plaque that described him as "the sole survivor of the Battle of the Little Bighorn" was removed in the 1970s at the request of local Native American tribes.

Auto detailers of the Old West

© Leigh Rubin

Comanche (pictured below) was considered "the sole survivor of the Battle of the Little Bighorn".

The last horse to be issued by the Army Quartermaster, and the last to carry the U.S. Army brand was a black colt foaled in Kansas in 1947 (on General Lee's birthday.) Named "Black Jack" after the nickname of General John Pershing, he was sent to the Third Infantry at Ft. Myer, Virginia. He was beautiful and restless, and was assigned to be the riderless horse with boots reversed in the stirrups that signified a fallen hero that follows the military caisson in military funerals. He was a fixture in more than 1,000 burial marches, including those of John F. Kennedy Jr., Herbert Hoover, and General Douglas McArthur.

This riderless horse follows the caisson bearing former President Ronald Reagan's flag-draped casket during his funeral procession.

The End of an Era

Sir Isaac Newton sketched a steam-driven wheeled vehicle in 1680, but it wasn't until 1769, in France, that the world's first self-propelled locomotive driven by steam was invented. The first combustion engine followed it in Switzerland in 1807, the four-stroke piston combustion engine in 1876, and by 1886, premier gasoline-powered automobiles were patented in Germany. Bicycles were in vogue in the 1890s as well, and by 1900 the "horseless carriage," the "tin Lizzie" (the automobile) began to be manufactured by hand, then by factory. By 1920, the gasoline engine had almost completely replaced the original animal's version of horsepower in the U.S.

"They said I was overqualified and that they only hire mules. Apparently, this place isn't an equine opportunity employer."

© Leigh Rubin

Horses in the U.S. were no longer an economic necessity after 1930. Draft horses were still used on some rural farms, but these too were almost all replaced by the 1950s. Today, horses are mostly used for pleasure riding, exhibition, and sport. Some are still employed on ranches and farms, or as police mounts, and horses still take people on trail rides in scenic locations, pull old-fashioned carriages in large cities, give hayrides and sleigh rides to "dudes" on private ranches, and entertain us on commercials during television shows, but most people do not encounter the horse on a daily basis or depend on its services any longer. But horses will always remind us of a time when man and animal depended on one another.

Horse Breeds

There are more than 300 recognized horse breeds found throughout the world. Breeds have fixed requirements for parentage, height, action, appearance, conformation, temperament, and usually color. There are light and heavy horse breeds, pony breeds, and miniature horses. Modern breeds are selectively bred for one or more human purpose such as halter, show, racing, driving, dressage, jumping, eventing, roping, reining, or endurance.

Some of the popular breeds in the U.S. are the Quarter Horse, the Thoroughbred, the Arabian, the Appaloosa, and the American Paint Horse. Mixed breed horses of unknown parentage are called "grade horses." Mixed breed horses may be less easily recognizable to the untrained eye, but can achieve just as high performance levels as purebreds given equal training and opportunity.

Where did all these horse breeds originate? Before humans rode horses, wild prototypical horses of different sizes roamed Europe and Asia. These horses were of four basic types depending on where they lived: The Hot, Dry Climate Desert Horse; the genetically smaller Desert Pony; the Cold, Wet Climate Forest Horse; and the smaller Forest Pony.

There were few flashy white "chrome" legs, easy-to-spot white faces, or loud patches on these early horses because foals born with mutations in color like these were easily preyed upon by hungry predators. Instead, tan horses with black manes, tails, and legs, or various shades of brown or dapple grey were the norm. Horses survived best when their coat color blended with the earth, the snow, the vegetation, or the dappled, dark shadows under trees.

The tiny Caspian is the second oldest horse breed still in existence today (the Asian Wild Horse is the oldest). The Caspian is a horse similar in type to the small, heat-resistant desert pony.

Once horses were domesticated, people started manipulating their reproduction, and the ancestors of today's modern breeds evolved. Humans delighted in lighter headed horses because they were easier on the arms while reining. Man also found that horses with big bottoms were excellent sprinters that could accelerate and turn quickly—and that these traits were useful for hunting purposes. Aesthetically, people liked prettier colors and some believed certain colors held special powers. Essentially, all horse traits were manipulated by man starting thousands of years ago. Temperament, color, speed, agility, strength, stamina—all were heightened or diminished depending on human need.

The Przewalski's Horse, also called the Asian Wild Horse, is one of the three "primitive" foundation horses (the Forest horse and the Tarpan are the other two). These horses were discovered by Colonel Nikolai Przewalski in 1879.

Inbreeding is defined as the mating of relatives. If an ancestor appears more than once in any one pedigree today, that animal is said to be inbred. An example of forced inbreeding is that all registered Thoroughbreds trace their origins to three stallions and about forty mares. Similarly, all registered Standardbreds trace their lineage to just one stallion. When a breed's studbook is closed to new sires, that breed is forced to be inbred. *Linebreeding* is the deliberate placement of one or two superior horses in the pedigrees of both mare and stallion for the likelihood of superior traits being passed to the foal.

The Thoroughbred evolved in England in the 17th and 18th centuries as a superior racehorse.

Some people think that if they breed dissimilar types together, they will get an average of the two, but this is not necessarily so. For instance, breeding a large horse with a small horse can give you a small horse with a really large head and plate-sized feet—not a pretty sight! It is better to breed horses similar in size, height, and substance to one another, and make sure there are no similar faults present in both, visual or genetic. Artificial insemination can help a breed improve because it enables a superior stallion to be bred to many unrelated mares, but it works only if they are of equal quality to him.

The American Mustang is descended from the Spanish horse that formed feral herds in the 16th century.
They are found in their largest numbers in the western United States.

The first Arabians imported to the U.S. arrived at the colony of Virginia in 1725. In 1873, Ulysses S. Grant was given two purebred Arabian stallions by a Turkish sultan, which resulted in the first Arabian breeding programs in the U.S. W.K. Kellogg (of the cereal fame) imported Crabbet Arabians, which were henceforth known as Crabbet-Kelloggs.

HOTBLOODS, COLDBLOODS, AND WARMBLOODS

Modern horses can be broken into two basic types: lighter, saddle or carriage horses, and the heavy agricultural breeds. The term "hotblood" is used to describe horses of a true, pure bloodline such as Arabians, Barbs, and Thoroughbreds. The term "coldblood" describes the heavy draft horses of Europe. Horses that have a mixture of the two are called "warmbloods." Hot- and warmbloods are typically long-legged with narrow bodies, while coldbloods have shorter, heavier legs, deep chests, and very large hooves.

The European Heavy Draft Horse breeds are called coldbloods, and are the huge, stoic, "easy keepers" with insulating fat layers under their thick skins. The Percheron, Clydesdale, Belgian, Shire, and to some extent the Friesian still resemble the northern European cold-blooded primitive type *Equus Robustus Steg* whose fossil remains show this horse prototype grew to 17 hands tall, and had six additional vertebrae compared to the pony-sized Tarpan of Mongolia. These gentle giants were concentrated in the extreme wet and cold northern European region of the Alps in Switzerland and Austria. Their heads and jaws were larger in proportion to their bodies, their hair was coarse and thick, and their manes and tails plentiful and often wavy. Their backs were long, their loins slanted and short, and they had thick "feathering" on the backs of their legs.

Draft breeds are still depended on by a few thousand Amish families in the U.S., and other traditional farmers worldwide. They are still able to deal with mud and snow better than machines, and they can go where no roads exist. They are used in tree farms to haul out selected logs without damaging or clearing any young trees in their path. An upsurge in interest in vaulting has meant more draft horses are being used for this sport today, and they have traditionally been used in circuses, parades, pulling contests, and to haul wagons and carriages giving old-fashioned rides.

Warmbloods (also known today as Sport Horses) are tall, elegant, expressive movers, Olympic team members, and superior equine athletes. The Warmblood was created by combining hot-blooded Thoroughbreds and Arabians with hardy native stock in Europe. Individual breeds with names like Hanoverian, Holsteiner, Oldenberg, and Trakehner indicate original Northern European heritage. Resulting later from crosses of Trakehners, Oldenburgs, Hanoverians, and additional Thoroughbred blood were the Bavarian Warmblood, the Belgian Warmblood, the Danish Warmblood, the Dutch Warmblood, and the Swedish Warmblood breeds.

"What do you mean you can't show us that one because it's not 'horse property'?! ... Why, that's downright discrimination!"

© Leigh Rubin

Warmbloods are typically used in dressage, hunter-jumper, eventing, and for driving. Their 16-hand and over stature, high leg action, upright, arched necks, and far-reaching stride make them impressive performers in the arena or field. From their primitive horse ancestors Warmbloods get substance and bone, from the Thoroughbred they get strenuous racing ability, galloping aptitude, and outstanding speed and performance, and from the Arabian, they get good temper, elegance, expressive heads, well-balanced proportions, and rapid regeneration after stress.

ANDALUSIAN

The Andalusian is descended from The Spanish Horse of the 1600s. It is also believed that the indigenous Sorraia of Portugal was used to create this breed. The prestigious schools of equestrian arts, and the fine military riding academies of Europe center around the majestic Andalusian and Lipizzaner breeds. In 1912, the title of "Pura Raza Espanola" was bestowed upon the Andalusian. The place of origin of these pure Spanish racehorses is said to be the Carthusian Monestary of Jerez, Spain.

The Andalusian shares the same genetic background as the Lusitano. The Andalusian is bred in the province of Andalusia in southern Spain, while the Lusitano is bred throughout Portugal.

The Andalusian's distinctive head often displays a convex profile. Its neck is well arched, though muscular and fairly short, and its legs have substantial bone and joints. The mane and tail are very thick and long, with the hair often wavy. The Andalusian is not a fast horse, but it is agile, athletic, and powerful. Today's Andalusians are used for pleasure, dressage, trail, and driving.

Most Andalusians are born dark, then lighten with age until they are pure white in their late teens. A few miss the dominant grey gene, however, and remain black or bay. Andalusians stand up to 15.2H.

ARABIANS

The Arabian Horse originally came from the deserts of the Middle East. It is one of the oldest basic horse types, easily recognizable, and clearly documented in art and literature from earliest recorded history. The word Arab or Arabia means "desert" or an inhabitant of the desert. There are several strains of Arabians. "Purebred Arabians" are considered to be "desert bred" lines, directly traceable back to the early Bedouin tribes. The Bedouins first bred Arabian horses, and shared their tents and food with these equine partners. This horse has a strong, lasting place in the hearts of many riders for their intelligence, agility, stamina, and fiery yet gentle nature.

The Arabian was ridden as early as 1500 BC. Mares were prized over stallions for raiding enemy tribes because mares showed great courage in battle, endured pain and injury without losing heart, and because they did not warn the enemy tribes by nickering to their horses as stallions do.

There are many different types of Arabians. The Shagya (named after the foundation sire) Arabian is heavier and taller, and was specifically bred to carry the Hungarian light cavalry in the 1800s. The Crabbet was bred in England directly from Egyptian desert-breds. The Polish, French, and Spanish Arabians descended partly from desert-breds and other types of Arabians mixed together.

Arabians have been introduced into most other horse breeds to add balanced athletic proportion, elegance, beauty, and general refinement. Arabians have a distinctive appearance that includes a long, arched neck, dished face, protruding large eyes, domed forehead (called a "jibbah"), horizontal croup, silky mane and tail, thin sensitive skin, short back, and long legs. Arabians have one less rib, one less lumbar bone, and two fewer tail bones than other horses, giving them a unique flat croup, very short back, and high set tail. Arabians possess a floating gait and springy step, are very fast and agile, and their graceful necks provide balance and flexibility. Their deep heart girth, large jaws, and large nostrils provide increased oxygen flow to their tissues, leading to greater stamina and rapid recovery after stress.

Arabians are ridden in most all disciplines, including racing, show, trail, pleasure, stock, dressage, and trial. A favorite class at Arabian shows is the costume class with its Americanized versions of beaded, flowing Bedouin garb. Arabians absolutely excel in endurance and distance riding.

Arabians stand from 14.1 to 15.3H, weigh from 800 to 1,200 pounds, and are found in most solid colors. Half Arabians are also registered, as are Morabs (Morgan Arabian cross), Anglo Arabs (Thoroughbred Arabian cross) and other combinations.

AZTECA

The Azteca is a recent breed from Mexico developed in 1972 by crossing Andalusian horses, Quarter Horses, and Criollos. The Azteca may have from three-eighths to a maximum of five-eighths Andalusian or Quarter Horse blood, with the Criollo blood not exceeding one-quarter. These horses are elegant, stand 15H to 16.1H high, have a straight or convex profile with expressive eyes and small ears. They have a short back, rounded croup, and medium to high withers, deep heart girth, hard hooves, strong legs, a silky coat, and full mane and tail. Only solid colors are acceptable.

The Azteca Horse Registry of America, incorporated in 1996, uses Andalusian stallions on Quarter Horse mares without the Criollo blood. Most U.S. Aztecas are grey, and stand 15.2 to 16H. They are said to mature slowly, and should not be ridden until age three.

The International Azteca Horse Association (IAzHA) was founded in 1992 to promote the breed. The horse is known for its elegant paces, and they do well with disciplines requiring collection such as dressage, ranch work, reining, cutting, team penning, pleasure riding, driving, polo, and trail.

BELGIAN

The Belgian Heavy Draft (known also as the Flanders or Brabant horse) is shorter and more squarely built than the other draft breeds. Their hooves are smaller, and the feathering on the backs of the legs more sparse. The Belgian is considered "pure draft" since it was not crossed as frequently with light horse breeds, so it still resembles the strong, stocky native mares mixed with the large, black Flemish Horses of medieval days.

The Belgian Heavy Draft horse was part of the development of many heavy breeds, including the Clydesdale and the Shire.

Since 1920 American breeders have bred only Belgians with sorrel, chestnut, or roan colors, all with flaxen manes and tails, short white socks, and white stripes down their faces. The Belgian Draft Horse Corporation of America was founded in Indiana in 1887. The breed enjoyed much growth in the U.S. in the 1920s and 30s, but the last imported Belgian was purchased in 1940. In 1980, the number of registrations climbed to over 4,000. In the U.S. today, there are more Belgians found than all other draft breeds combined. The Belgian is docile, kind, and an avid worker that does not enjoy idleness. They stand 16 to 18H high, and weigh between 1,800 and 2,000 pounds.

CLYDESDALE

The Clydesdale comes from the region around the Clyde River in Scotland where local mares with the "sabino" coloration were bred with black Flemish stallions. The sabino is a white pinto pattern that consistently produces tall white legs from knee or hock down, an excessively white or "bald face," and a white spot on the belly (originally considered to represent purity of the breed) which sometimes extends high onto the sides of the horse.

In contrast to other heavy draft breeds, the leaner Clydesdale was created for less sheer bulk and power, and more for agility and docility combined with strength and size. At 16 to 19H, and from 1,600 to 2,200 pounds, the Clydesdale stands at six feet tall or over. It was traditionally used for coal, agricultural, and haulage uses in its native land before being imported here in large numbers in the 1800s.

In 1933 the Clydesdale Breeders of the USA was incorporated. That same year was fortuitous for the breed when August Busch, Jr. gave his father, a partner in the beer company Anheuser-Busch, a gift of a six-horse team of Clydesdales. With their flashy color, high leg action, and long stride they publicly delivered a case of Budweiser Beer to President Roosevelt at the White House when Prohibition was repealed. They became the corporate trademark of that beer company and are still visible on television commercials and in exhibitions today.

"For the last time, Hubert, sometimes 'whoa!' really *does* mean 'whoa!'"

© Leigh Rubin

In 1937 an equine sleeping sickness epidemic—plus the introduction of the rubber-tired tractors—significantly reduced the numbers and use of all draft breeds to an all-time low, but the Clydesdales were helped by the continued importation, breeding, and showing of the Budweiser team. Today, the recognized bay sabino-colored Clydesdales (and solid colors as well) are found in parades, shows, dressage, hunter-jumper events, trail, and therapeutic riding programs. They are proudly considered the "only" draft breed in the country of Scotland.

The Clydesdale is a relatively new breed, having originated in the early 18th century.

Friesian

The Friesian Horse is found in records dating back to the 1200s. Originally bred using *Equus Robustus* in the province of Friesland in Northern Holland, the solid black, cold-blooded heavy draft was crossed with the Spanish Andalusian to create a unique "warmblooded" draft horse. With no white allowed on legs or body except a small star on the forehead, the Friesian is shorter and less bulky than the other draft breeds of Europe, but still possesses the characteristic long, flowing, wavy mane and tail, and feathers on the backs of its legs.

Traditionally, Friesians were used for agriculture, carriage, war, heavy draft, pleasure riding, and in the circus. With its tall, romantic appearance, high knee action, small head and arched neck, the Friesian is ridden today in dressage exhibitions and horse theater.

The Dutch brought their favorite horse with them when they settled New Amsterdam in 1625. After the English took possession and renamed this area New York, the Friesian breed was lost in North America. In 1974 the Friesian Horse Association of North America (FHANA), acting as a representative of the official Dutch Friesch Paarden Stamboek (FPS), the Dutch parent studbook founded in 1879, reintroduced the Friesian to North America. Today, the FPS has 45,000 registered Friesians worldwide, with 4,000 of them in North America. Friesians are carefully inspected, tested and rated before being allowed to register to ensure highest quality.

HANOVERIAN

The Hanoverian comes from the Northern German state of Lower Saxony, in the former kingdom of Hannover. The first studbook on this breed was opened in 1735, when Thoroughbreds were crossed with local mares to produce a horse with robust carriage and substantial bone that was sturdy and full of stamina for harness and military use.

The American Hanoverian Society was incorporated in the U.S. in 1978, and today this noble horse with cooperative temperament, elastic gaits, and correct conformation places well in performance sports. Hanoverians won 13 medals in the 1992 Olympics, and five gold, one silver, and two bronze in show jumping and dressage in the 1996 Olympics. In order for a horse to be registered, both American and German judges must carefully inspect, test, and rate the animal to determine its eligibility. All solid colors are acceptable. The Hanoverian stands around 16.2H on average.

The Hanoverian is the most numerous of the European warmbloods. It is often used in dressage.

Traditionally a powerful carriage horse, today's Holsteiners are among the world's best show jumpers.

HOLSTEINER

Holsteiner breeding has been going on since the thirteenth century in the northernmost province of Germany, Schleswig-Holstein. Native stock crossed with Neapolitan, Spanish, and Oriental horses started this breed, and in the nineteenth century, the Yorkshire Coach Horse and Thoroughbred were added as more emphasis was put on a riding horse rather than a coach horse.

The Holsteiner is a bold jumper, and has a tractable, intelligent, and reliable nature. Standing 16 to 17H, the traditional color for this breed has been bay with no or few white markings.

LIPIZZANER

The Lipizzaner was first bred by Archduke Charles II for his father, the Austrian Emperor Ferdinand I in 1580, and traces its roots directly to the famed Spanish Horse. Bred originally in Lipizza (hence the name), they are now bred at a stud farm in Piber, Austria, and also in Hungary, Romania, and the former Czechoslovakia.

The Lipizzaner is described as a "rectangular" horse with a long, powerful back, muscular croup, low withers, powerful head, wide chest, upright short shoulders, shorter legs, hard feet, and dense bone. They remain fit and sound for many years, still working while in their twenties and thirties. Used originally as a carriage horse, this classic dressage horse is famous for its "airs above the ground" leaps and kicks, which were used for offensive military purposes at one time. The Lipizzaner is a slow maturing breed, often not finished growing until seven years old. Lipizzaners stand between 15.1 and 16.2H.

Today, Lipizzaners at the Spanish Riding School in Vienna, Austria, give public performances in the baroque riding halls where these pure white horses and their riders dressed in brown give a small taste of their training, performing such skills as the Pas de Deux ("dance for two"), where pairs of riders perform side by side to traditional music.

MOROCCAN BARB

The Moroccan Barb originated in the Maghreb region on the Barbary Coast of Northern Africa. It is a primitive, basic horse proto-type. The Moroccan Barb's thick body, powerfully muscled hindquarters, flat withers, sturdy legs and hooves, and large coarse head do not make it a particularly attractive horse, but the Barb possesses vigor, hardiness, reliability, and is a fast sprinter over short distances. The Barb is reputed to have a fiery, unpredictable temperament and to be a spirited mount for skilled riders only.

The "Godolphin Arabian" (also known as the "The Coke Barb") was one of the three foundation sires of all Thoroughbreds, and was said not to be an Arabian at all, but a Moroccan Barb, a horse of only 14H, with a plain head and muscular hindquarters. The Moroccan Barb contributed its genes to the Spanish Lippizaner, Andalusian, and Lusitano. The Moroccan Barb of today stands up to 15.2H, and is found in most solid colors.

"Personally, I don't see how they get any rest at all sleeping like that."

© Leigh Rubin

Norwegian Fjord

From the Vikings in Norway comes the Norwegian Fjord Horse, a short, round 13 to 14.2H equine whose distinctive appearance centers around its powerful body, dun coloration, and distinctive upright mane. Resembling the Mongolian ass-like wild Przewalski's Horse in coloration, body type, and mane (and some say temperament), the Fjord Horse was also combined with other ancient pony types to produce today's surefooted, heavy-shouldered, riding and driving horse.

A hardy, long-lived, easy keeper able to survive extremes of temperature, the dun factor coloration produces a light yellow, grey, whitish, or tan with primitive dorsal striping down the back, into the mane and tail, and on the legs. The Norwegian Fjord's mane is traditionally cut short in an upraised arch over the neck, with the outer white hairs shorter than the inner dark dorsal stripe hairs producing an interesting, bi-colored, upright crest. Weighing 900 to 1,200 pounds, these robust animals love attention and are happiest when working. The Norwegian Fjord Horse Registry was established in the U.S. in 1949 to ensure breeding quality of these stout, colorful, small horses.

The Norwegian Fjord bears the closest resemblance to the Asian Wild Horse of the Ice Age.

Oldenburgs are usually brown, black, or bay.

OLDENBURG

The Oldenburg was bred in the former kingdom of Oldenburg in northern Germany. The breed was developed in the seventeenth century using Friesian mares and Spanish and Italian stallions to produce a grand carriage horse. Then in the early 1960s the German Oldenburg Breeding Association crossed Oldenburg mares with Thoroughbred stallions to further refine the breed, producing a modern riding horse and an outstanding sport horse.

The Oldenburg has a fine head, long neck, long shoulders, strong back and loin, and well-muscled legs. It stands between 16.2 and 17.2H. Oldenburgs mature earlier than other warmbloods. They are frequently used in show jumping today.

Paso Fino

The Paso Fino is said to be descended from The Spanish Jennet, a horse from the 1600s with smooth gaits. The Paso Fino (which means "fine walk") gait is a four-beat, lateral (pacing) gait that occurs naturally from birth in which there is very little up and down movement of topline. Its speed increases from the *paso fino* gait to the *paso corto* to the *paso largo*, but the rider stays motionless in the saddle. (This is called the Flat Walk in other gaited breeds.) The Paso Fino is versatile and adapts well to a variety of climates and purposes. The National Paso Fino Horse Association was established in 1992.

The Paso Fino is originally from Puerto Rico, and is a direct derivative of the Peruvian Paso.

Paso Finos have relatively small ears that curve inward at the tips, and are set on a well-shaped, alert, and intelligent head. This horse has a gracefully arched neck, sloping shoulders, deep heart girth, low withers, short muscled back, slightly sloping croup with rounded hips, strong yet refined legs, sloping medium pasterns, and a long, luxurious mane and tail. Paso Finos stand from 13 to 15.2H, weigh 700 to 1,100 pounds, and come in every color imaginable. They are spirited and responsive under saddle, but sensible and gentle at hand.

The Paso Fino is very popular in the United States.

PERUVIAN PASO

The Peruvian Paso was bred in South America from horses brought over by the conquistadors, and is considered the "National Horse of Peru" today. Created from the Spanish Jennet and the Moroccan Barb, this horse has a smooth, ambling gait and great stamina. The Peruvian Paso has a gait called the "termino" with high, outward movements of the front legs. As with the Paso Fino, this horse exhibits "brio," or enthusiastic vigor, that enables it to travel for many hours and miles in the service of its rider. The Peruvian Paso Horse Registry of North America was established in 1970, but in 2004 it consolidated with the North American Peruvian Horse Association.

The Peruvian Paso is somewhat larger than the Paso Fino, and its stride is longer. Standing between 14.1 and 15.2H, it comes in chestnut, black, brown, bay, buckskin, palomino, grey, dun, and roan. The mane is abundant with fine thick hair that may be wavy or straight.

The Peruvian Paso can move at a steady 11 miles per hour for long periods over rough and rugged terrain.

PERCHERON

The Percheron comes from the Perche region of France. They were most often bred to be grey (although other colors are acceptable today) so they were more visible at night when pulling coaches. Muscled and tall at 15 to 19H and up to 2,600 pounds (with the average being 1,900) these horses were also able to trot seven to ten miles per hour day in and out. They were used to pull carriages, aid in warfare, haul for the coal and timber industry, and help with the harvest.

Edward Harris of Moorestown, New Jersey, first imported Percherons to the United States in 1839. In his two attempts to import eight Percheron horses to America, only two survived the journey, a mare named Joan and a stallion called Diligence. These two horses helped establish the Percheron breed in America.

The Percheron Horse Association of America was formed in 1934 after the breed was imported here in the 1800s in great numbers. During the Great Depression, the draft horse made a rural comeback due to lack of gasoline for tractors, but after 1940 when gas was plentiful again, their numbers declined dramatically. Only the Amish farmers depended on the draft horse for their livelihood. In 1954 there were only 85 Percherons registered in the PHAA, but today the numbers have risen to around 3,000. Their uses include romantic city transportation, old-fashioned sleigh and hayrides in the country, medieval jousting, vaulting, farming, circus, pleasure riding, and event jumping.

SHIRE

The word "shire" comes from an old Saxon word "schyran," which means to shear or divide, and this came to mean any county in England. In the 1700s, the Shire horse was known as "The Old English Black Horse" throughout England. Standing from 16.2 to 19H, the horse was tall, strong, and big-barreled, but with a finer, smaller head for its size. Many old photos of famous Shire stallions from the 1800s consistently show huge, attractive, solid black horses with two hind white socks, and a long white blaze that extended over the nose and sometimes onto the chin.

Shires were improved with Friesian blood, and imported into the U.S. in great numbers in the late 1800s. One roan stallion named "Great Britain" still weighed over 2,800 pounds after a week at sea! The average Shire is said to weigh a ton and able to move five tons. The American Shire Horse Association was incorporated in 1885. Importation stopped completely in 1939, but isolated herds (barely) kept the breed alive in the U.S. Today, shows and classes featuring the "heavies" of the equine world, including the Shire, consistently draw large numbers of spectators. They are acceptable in black, bay, brown, and grey, but excessive white and roaning are considered undesirable.

The massive Shire is one of the biggest horses in the world. The tallest and heaviest Shire was a gelding named Samson, foaled in England in 1846, who stood 21.2 hands high, and weighed 3,360 pounds at maturity.

THOROUGHBRED

The Thoroughbred racehorse originated in the seventeenth and eighteenth centuries in Great Britain when approximately 35 native sprinting mares (possibly Scottish Galloways) were bred to three select, imported desert stallions. Thoroughbreds are the fastest horses—they have long legs and tall, thin bodies perfect for racing. Thoroughbreds have been used to improve a multitude of other breeds over the years in the areas of speed, stamina, and height.

The first Thoroughbred foundation sire imported to the U.S. was Bulle Rock who was brought to the colony of Virginia in 1730. The second important foundation stallion was Lexington from Maryland who dominated the bloodlines through the nineteenth century. Although informal Thoroughbred racing was held earlier, the first recognized race in America was held at Annapolis, Maryland, in 1745.

From license fees and taxes, Thoroughbred racing generates nearly $500 million in U.S. government revenue every year today. Approximately 35,000 Thoroughbred foals are registered each year in the U.S., with the largest number coming from Kentucky, Florida, and California.

All of the horses used in the sport of Steeplechasing are Thoroughbreds whose lineage must be proven.

Thoroughbreds are the fastest horses on earth.

The Jockey Club ensures the pedigree of Thoroughbreds in the U.S., and today its computer database holds the names of three million horses, and the daily results of every Thoroughbred race in America and worldwide. From the late 1970s until 2000, every foal registered and its sire and dam were DNA blood-typed to prove parentage claims, but beginning with the foal crop of 2001, mane and tail hair samples replaced blood as DNA verification.

Yearling race horses are sold at auction or kept by their breeders. A racehorse begins training as a yearling, learning to accept a saddle and bridle, then a rider on its back, and to break from the starting gate and run around the track.

The typical Thoroughbred stands 16H tall, and is bay, brown, chestnut, black, grey, or roan in color. White is confined to the face and below the knees. The neck is long, head refined, withers high and defined, and the shoulders deep and extremely sloped and well muscled. The heart girth is deep but relatively narrow, the thigh is long, and the hip powerful. Some Thoroughbreds are high strung and have difficult temperaments, but they are competitive and courageous to the extreme. Thoroughbreds excel in jumping, three-day eventing, steeplechase, fox hunting, polo, and other competitive, fast, demanding disciplines.

A number of famous racehorses were large, such as Man O' War and Secretariat, but smaller ones like War Admiral, Seabiscuit (pictured below), Northern Dancer, and Smarty Jones were just as famous and fast.

TRAKEHNER

In 1872 in an area once known as East Prussia, the Trakehner breed was created in the Trakehnen region in 1732. Since World War II, this fine carriage, cavalry, farm, and performance horse has been bred in West Germany. They are a horse of great substance and bone that are anxious to please. They have a springy floating trot, and soft, balanced canter.

A keen, elegant, balanced jumper and all around athlete, this breed stands 16 to 17H. The Trakehner has Arabian and Thoroughbred blood as well as hardy, small, native Schweiken stock in its lineage. A slow maturing horse, the Trakehner should not be ridden before the age of three because its own body weight is so great that it does not need the additional burden of a rider stressing its developing joints.

Trakehners have been consistent Olympic medal winners in dressage, eventing, and jumping since 1924. In 1936, the Trakehner-dominated German team won every medal at the Olympic games. In the 1950s, Canada first began importing these horses to their country, then the U.S. followed suit.

In 1974, the American Trakehner Association was established, and great care has been taken to preserve these horses.

Small Horses and Ponies

Ponies are basically small horses. The word "pony" is derived from the French word "poulenet," which means a foal. The proportions of a pony are what make it unique. Ponies have long bodies and short legs, as compared to larger horse breeds that have long legs that are in proportion to the length of their bodies.

Popular breeds of ponies standing from around 11H to 14.2H include the Shetland, Welsh, and Hackney. Small horses like the Halflinger, the Icelandic, and the Norwegian Fjord provide adults with strong, willing mounts of unimposing height, but no less stamina and heart than larger horses. The American Mustang also often falls into the 13H to 14.2H category.

Welsh Ponies

Halflinger

HACKNEY PONY

The Hackney Pony was derived from the British Fell Pony, the Welsh Mountain Pony, and the Hackney Horse. The breed was created in the 1880s with the foundation sire Sir George of Cumbria. The word "Hackney" comes originally from the French "*haquenee*," which means a horse for hire. This gave rise to the word "hack" as a drudge, and "hackneyed" as overused or trite.

The Hackney Pony was created by Christopher Wilson of Cumbria in the 1880s; they were first called "Wilson Ponies."

Hackneys have very high leg action at the trot, and with their upright necks and highset tails look very elegant in harness. Most Hackney Ponies today are show harness horses with their explosive motion and brilliant manner. Their leg action at the trot is so high that they appear to be in suspended animation, often touching their upper bodies with their upraised hooves, which move with piston-like precision. As show ponies they are hitched to a four-wheeled buggy called a Viceroy, or worked in two pairs pulling a miniature stage coach. When hitched in two pairs, the wheelers should be larger than the leaders, whose job it is to be showy and quick. Hackney Ponies were imported to the U.S. in 1872 with a mare named Stella 239. In 1891 the American Hackney Horse Society was formed.

HALFLINGER

The Halflinger originates from a race of heavy draft ponies found in the Southern Tyrolean Alps of present day Austria and Northern Italy mixed with an Arabian stallion and other native pony breeds. A short, robust, chestnut-colored horse, it was used for traversing the steep mountain trails of this region. It is named after the village of Hafling. All registered Austrian Haflingers have an Edelweiss brand on them with the letter H. All modern purebred Haflingers must trace their lineage directly to one foundation sire, named 249 Folie.

Haflingers are always chestnut colored with flaxen mane and tail.

During World War II, Haflingers were used as pack horses by the military, but after the war they were further refined for riding and driving. The first Haflingers arrived in the U.S. in 1958, and today the breed is used for draft, driving, pleasure, trail, endurance, dressage, jumping, and vaulting.

Standing 13.3 to 14.3H, the horse's appearance should be well-muscled with clean, correct limbs, a refined expressive head with large eyes, and a croup not too steep or too short. The American Haflinger Registry was formed in 1998.

ICELANDIC

The Icelandic Horse, with its unique flying pace and tölt gaits stands at a non-threatening and an easy-to-mount height of between 12.3 and 13.2H. This athletic dynamo can carry adults easily over the ground with its special fast tölt gait, which can keep up with other horses moving at a gallop. The tölt is a smooth, four-beat gait with a high foreleg action, and a dignified headset (similar to the running walk in the American Gaited breeds.) The Icelandic can also master an extremely fast two-beat pace called a "skeid" where two legs on one side of the body move together in unison, akin to the way American Standardbreds pace at high speeds.

Since the year 1,100, the import of any horses to Iceland has been forbidden.

Originally brought to Iceland by the Norse in longboats between 860 and 935 AD, Icelandics have not been crossed with any other breed for one thousand years. The horses are pastured outside in wild herds and not started in training until age four. They live long healthy lives for 25 to 30 years, and live beyond 40.

Today there are 70,000 Icelandics registered in other countries, and 80,000 in Iceland. Long distance horse trekking is a popular tourist activity in Iceland on these little mounts. The U.S. Icelandic Horse Congress maintains the U.S. Registry.

SHETLAND PONY

The small yet strong Shetland Pony is an ancient breed that originates from the Shetland Isles off the north coast of Scotland. Standing only 40 inches (10H) tall at the withers, it was derived from the Scandinavian Tundra Horse, a prehistoric wetlands pony type suitable for surviving extreme cold and precipitation with its heavy mane and tail, dense coarse body hair, feathers on backs of its legs, and retention of body fat.

In the nineteenth century, Shetlands were used in the coalmines of Europe and the U.S. as "pit ponies" because they were small, strong, and tractable enough to fit into the tunnels to carry out the ore.

The first import of Shetlands to the U.S. occurred in 1885. In America, they were crossed with the Hackney Pony to create the American Shetland, and with the Appaloosa to create the Pony of the Americas.

Shetland Ponies were first used to carry peat and for ploughing. Then, in the mid-19th century, when laws were passed prohibiting children from working in coal mines, thousands of Shetlands travelled to Southern Britain to be 'pit ponies,' working underground their whole lives hauling coal.

MINIATURE HORSES

Miniature Horse

Miniature Horses were created in Europe as pets for the nobility in the 1600s. The American Miniature Horse standards of today specify that Minis be refined-looking, have good conformation, and possess well-proportioned features similar to those of a regular-sized horse. Dwarfism, a recessive gene carrying with it a variety of birth defects and undesirable traits, is found in miniature horses due to the past practice of deliberately using dwarf stallions to reduce the size of minis. Today's Minis can carry one hidden dwarfish gene with no outward show.

There are two categories for size of the Miniature Horse in the American Miniature Horse Registry (established in 1978). Division A has a height of no more than 34" at the "last hair of the mane," and Division B measures 34" to 38" at the same point. The American Miniature Horse Association, also formed in 1978, recognizes only horses in Division A, or at 34" or less.

Miniature Horses are particularly non-threatening and lovable due to their size—especially the foals, who are born at 15" to 22" high, and weigh only 12 to 25 pounds.

WELSH PONIES

The Welsh Pony types evolved in the hills of Wales in southwestern Great Britain. The Romans introduced Arabian and Barb blood, and the pony became more refined and beautiful, but still retained the stamina and hardiness of the native stock. Today's Welsh Mountain Pony (known as the Section A) is the smallest of the Welsh equines, standing at under 12.2H.

Larger still is the Welsh Pony Cob Type, or Section C, which is heavier and thicker bodied and can also be used for packing, harness, trail riding, farming, dressage, and hunter-jumper.

All Welsh Ponies have tough hooves, are said to be intelligent and easy to train, have large, bold eyes, small heads, short backs, strong quarters, high-set tails, fine hair, and laid back shoulders. They are acceptable in all colors but pinto.

Crossing Welsh Cobs (the larger riding horses of Wales) and Arabians with Welsh Mountain Ponies produced the larger Welsh Pony. Standing under 14.2H, this is called the Section B type in the Welsh Pony and Cob Society of America, which was established in 1907. The Welsh Pony is used for driving, and all performance disciplines for children.

Welsh Pony

AMERICAN BREEDS

Some of the most popular breeds today that were "Made in the USA" are the Appaloosa, American Paint Horse, the Pinto Horse, American Quarter Horse, American Morgan, Tennessee Walking Horse, Rocky Mountain Horse, Missouri Fox Trotter, American Mustang, American Saddlebred, Spotted Saddle Horse, Palomino, American Bashkir Curly, American Miniature Horse, American Cream Draft, and the Pony of the Americas.

Since there were no modern horses residing in the U.S. prior to the 1500s all American horse breeds were created using imported stock. Separate American registries were created, or offshoots to European registries made in the U.S. so that standards and rules could uphold the quality and appearance of the emerging American horse breeds.

American mustangs

Today the American Quarter Horse has the highest number of animals registered worldwide, with around three million. Many other American breeds are very popular internationally as well. The U.S. holds the distinction of having the largest and most varied selection of breeds in one country today.

American Paint Horse, and Pinto

The American Paint and the Pinto refer to a variety of horse breeds and mixed breeds with specific coat colorizations. The Spanish word "pintado" means painted, and this was anglicized into the word "pinto" then "paint" by early Americans. (The British call a black and white coat "piebald," and a white and any other color coat "skewbald.")

Tobiano refers to a coat pattern where the coat is white with large patches of solid color. Overo is a coat pattern in which the coat is colored with patches of white that almost never cross the back.

In 1956 The Pinto Horse Association (PtHA) was incorporated, followed by the American Paint Horse Association (APHA) in 1965. Besides bloodline and conformation registry rules, there are two major white patterns (over any solid-colored base) recognized by Paint Horse breeders: tobiano and overo. (A mixture of these two, called "Tovero," often shows more white than either pattern.)

American Paint Horses register only the offspring of horses with Paint, Quarter Horse, or Thoroughbred papers, whereas the Pinto Horse can be any breed that meets the color requirement. Paint and Pinto horses are ridden in most disciplines such as pleasure riding, stock management, show, rodeo, jumping, and trail riding, and stand approximately 14.2 to 16H.

APPALOOSA

The Appaloosa breed was created in the eighteenth century by the Nez Perce Indians of the North American Pacific Northwest. The Appaloosa traits and coloration can be found in any breed, but the Appaloosa breed was officially established in the Palouse River area (hence the name Appaloosa from the term "a Palouse horse" or "a Palousey") from Spanish horses brought into the area in the 1700s.

In 1877, when their peace treaty was broken, the Nez Perce were forced out of their homeland and most of their valuable horses were lost or destroyed. The breed was revived in 1938 by a wheat farmer who started the Appaloosa Horse Club (ApHC) in Idaho. In less than fifty years, the Appaloosa breed registry became the third largest in the world.

Breed characteristics of the Appaloosa are mottled skin on the lips and genitals, sparse mane and tail, white sclera around the eyes which gives them a more human-like appearance, vertically striped hooves, and five recognized coat patterns of the white blanket, marble, leopard, snowflake, and frost roan over a darker base coat.

The appearance of an Appaloosa's color can change dramatically throughout one horse's lifetime. They are used for many disciplines including pleasure riding, stock management, trail, and jumping. They stand anywhere from 14.2 to 16H.

BASHKIR CURLY

Established in 1971, The American Bashkir Curly Registry sought to protect this unique horse with the poodle-like curly coat. Originating in Russia, the Bashkir Curly found its way into wild, and then American Indian horse herds in the 1800s in the Western United States.

Originally known as the native Lokai breed in Russia, this small, stocky, predominately chestnut-colored horse stood around 14H, and lived in the foothills of the Ural Mountains. It was kept outside in herds in subzero temperatures, surviving the deep snow by growing a dense curly coat (which could be spun to make clothing.) A pair of Bashkirs were reputed to be able to pull a sleigh 75 to 85 miles in 24 hours without being fed.

Bashkir Curly foals are born with their thick, curly coats, including kinky manes, tails, eyelashes, and even curly ear hair! The mane, tail, and wavy coat are shed seasonally. Bashkir Curlies can be used for many disciplines involving strength and toughness, and are enjoying popularity today for their docile, easy-to-train temperaments as well as their unusual appearance. These modern, American Bashkir Curlies no longer resemble the Bashkir Horses of Russia.

AMERICAN CREAM DRAFT

The American Cream Draft Horse is the only draft breed to originate in the U.S. The breed's foundation mare "Old Granny" was recognized in 1911. The American Cream Draft Horse Association, created in 1944, set its color standards as cream color with a pink skin, white mane and tail, and amber to light reddish brown eyes. Foals are born with nearly white eyes that turn amber at one year of age.

This breed has among its sires Yancy No. 3 out of a black Percheron mare that attained a weight of 1,600 pounds, and Silver Lace out of a sorrel Belgian mare of 2,000 pounds (who contributed increased size to his progeny.) The best cream color comes from mating two creams with pink skins together. Darker skins do not produce the desired shades. The special combination of pink skin, amber eyes, and a light gold body with white mane and tail are indicative of the presence of the champagne allele, which is a rare color variation, in this breed's case, of a sorrel, or light chestnut colored horse. Old Granny was able to pass on to her offspring quite often (no matter the sire's color) her champagne coloration.

American Cream Draft stallions weigh from 1,800 to 2,000 pounds, and mares from 1,600 to 1,800 pounds. These horses stand from 15 to 16.3H.

AMERICAN "GAITED" HORSES

The term "gaited horse" refers to those breeds that possess natural gaits (other than the normal horse walk, trot, and canter) that cause less up and down jarring movement of the horse's back and legs for increased rider comfort. These horses have a long hip (30% of body length or more), lowered hindquarters, an angle of the pelvis that is neither too steep nor completely flat, a long horizontal shoulder, and the ratio of their rear leg bones to each other is about the same, producing a long hind leg capable of a low, sliding over stride exceeding the tracks of the front feet. The smooth, low action of the front legs matches it, and their rather long necks are set low on their bodies so that their heads nod in time to their hoofbeats. Gaited horses excel in endurance, pleasure riding, trail, show, and driving. They are also popular with older horseback riders who desire a little more comfort on their journey. Gaited breeds include the Saddlebred, Missouri Fox Trotter, Rocky Mountain Horse, Spotted Saddle Horse, and the Tennessee Walker.

MISSOURI FOX TROTTERS

Missouri Fox Trotters were created in the Ozark Mountains by settlers in the 1800s from the Spanish horse, the Morgan, and the Saddlebred who wanted smooth-gaited, surefooted horses to haul logs, work cattle, pull the plow and the carriage, and also be suitable for pleasure riding over long distances on narrow, rugged mountain trails. Fox Trotters have three special gaits: the "flat walk," the faster "running walk," and the slow, rolling "rocking horse" canter. The flat walk and running walk are four-beat diagonal "fox trots," which consist of trotting with the hind legs while walking with the front.

The Missouri Fox Trotting Horse Breed Association was incorporated in 1958 in Missouri where it is still headquartered today. This horse is the state horse of Missouri.

AMERICAN MORGAN

The American Morgan Horse had as its first foundation stallion a bay colt named Figure born in 1789 in Vermont and owned by teacher and horseman Justin Morgan. This horse was worked hard at the plow, hauled timber, cleared woodlands, was matched in severe weight-pulling contests, and was raced in harness and under saddle. His breeding was never officially established, but he was thought to have been sired by the Thoroughbred True Briton, or else by a Friesian or Welsh Cob import. Nevertheless, Figure was in high demand as a sire and all present-day Morgan Horses are traced to him and his sons.

By 1894, "The Justin Morgan Horse" had so many breeders that they joined together to establish the first "Morgan Horse Register" to record lineage and set standards for the breed.

Morgans have been historically used as record-setting trotters, the finest Cavalry mounts, proud driving horses, and for all types of English and Western riding disciplines. The Morgan Horse contributed foundation stock to other American breeds such as the Standardbred, Saddlebred, and the Tennessee Walking Horse.

Morgan Horses are known for their muscled, compact bodies, upright graceful necks, small ears above a broad forehead, expressive eyes, and their general versatility, intelligence, stamina, and willingness to work. They stand between 14.2 and 15.2H.

American Morgan Horse

MUSTANGS

The word "mustang" is a corruption of the word "mestana," which means a herd of horses, and is used to describe the wild horses of the United States. Mustangs descended from the Spanish horses brought to America in the 1500s, and at the start of the twentieth century, there were approximately one million wild horses roaming the open rangelands of the American west. Their population today is roughly 45,000 animals, with most living on Bureau of Land Management (BLM) Herd Management Areas (HMA) in ten western states.

American Mustangs or "BLM Mustangs" of many mixed breeds can resemble anything from Percherons to Morgans to Welsh Ponies, depending on the history of the Herd Management Area (HMA) and what was released in, or strayed to, that area. Generally known for their superior stamina, toughness, intelligence, agility, and "hybrid vigor," nature dictates that only those individuals possessing superior survival skills live through their rugged, isolated upbringing.

Kiger Mustangs are descendants from a certain group of BLM mustangs from the Kiger and Riddle BLM Herd Management Areas in the Steens Mountains of southeastern Oregon.

Many Native Americans believed that certain horses were protected by the placement of dark-colored "shields" over their heads, eyes, chest, flanks, and croups, and called these horses Medicine Hat pintos, believing that "big medicine" or magical protection occurred to horse and rider in battle.

The Marine Corps Mounted Color Guard (the only remaining U.S. Mounted Color Guard existing today) rides nothing but palomino-colored American Mustangs gentled and trained by the soldiers.

PALOMINO

The Palomino Horse Breeders Association was incorporated in the U.S. in 1941 to recognize golden horses with white manes and tails of certain breeds. Palomino is a color, not a type, which according to the PHBA presents itself as "variations of a 14 karat gold coin." Mane and tail of registered Palominos must be white with no more than 15 percent dark hairs included. The word Palomino comes from the Spanish word "palo," from the Latin "pallere," to be pale. The Palomino Fino is also the name of a golden Spanish grape.

Any horse can have the palomino coloration. Palomino is a genetically diluted "cream" version of reddish brown; the common "chestnut" or "sorrel" horse color. The lightest variation of Palomino is called "Isabella" in honor of Queen Isabella of Spain, who is said to have worn a white silk blouse that yellowed to this color during Spain's historic long siege of Ostende.

Palomino horses are found in all breeds, and used for all disciplines especially parade, show, trail, rodeo, and pleasure riding.

PONY OF THE AMERICAS

These colorful mounts were the result of one colt (born to an Arab-Appaloosa mare accidentally bred to a Shetland Pony stallion) given to a lawyer and Shetland pony breeder in Iowa. The colt was white with black markings that looked like a hand on his flank, so he was called Black Hand. The lawyer was so impressed with this colt that he established him as the foundation sire for the Pony of the Americas Club (POA Club) that he started in 1956.

At that time, the standards for a registered Pony of the Americas were a 52" height maximum, a small, dish-faced, Arabian-type head, a muscled body, Appaloosa coloration visible at 40 feet, and a gentle, easy-to-train temperament suitable for children to train, ride, and show. In 1986 the maximum height allowable increased to 56" due to taller ponies becoming more desirable. There are over 40,000 registrants in the POA Club.

Adults in POA shows are only allowed to show ponies at halter, or drive them in harness. The POA is the only club designed to promote the confidence and abilities of young riders alone. The POA motto is, "Try hard, win humbly, lose gracefully, and, if you must… protest with dignity."

Pony of the Americas

The Quarter Horse is recognized in thirteen solid colors with white markings restricted to the face and below the knees.

AMERICAN QUARTER HORSE

The first "all-American breed," the Quarter Horse was created in the seventeenth century from a mixture of Colonial Spanish, cold-blooded, and Native American mares bred with imported English Thoroughbreds (notably Janus and Sir Archy). The first horse of Quarter Horse type (before the name and breed existed) that attracted a good deal of attention was Steel Dust, who was foaled in 1843. He stood 15H high and weighed around 1,200 pounds. He was popular as a running horse, and sired many running and cow horses that were known as "Steel Dust horses." Peter McCue, a stallion foaled in 1895, and later Joe Hancock, Old Sorrel, and Three Bars were influential early sires as well.

The Quarter Horses' short, muscular build, broad back, large hindquarters, agile legs, and speed of sprint from standing start enables them to run a quarter of a mile in approximately 20 seconds (hence the name), and their smooth gaits, gentleness, and intelligence helped Western and Southwestern cowboys to rope, herd, and ride the range more comfortably and productively. Quarter Horses were bred for their "cow sense," meaning they anticipate and follow the movements of cattle with little or no cues from the rider, and have the desire and ability to outmaneuver a cow to keep it cut from the rest of the herd.

Dale Evans was from Texas but could not ride a horse, at first, and had to take lessons in Hollywood. Her horse, Buttermilk, was a light buckskin Quarter Horse originally named Taffy that was rescued from a slaughterhouse. Buttermilk was so fast out of the starting block that Trigger, with Roy Rogers on board, often appeared left behind as Dale sped away to the rescue, which required frequent retakes, and irked Roy.

A "Foundation Quarter Horse" is one that was listed in the first five studbooks, or in the first 27,000 horses registered—or one that carries at least 80 percent Foundation blood today. Appendix Horses are Thoroughbred-Quarter Horse crosses of any percentage. Appendix Horses have more Thoroughbred traits than Foundation Quarter Horses, such as higher withers, thinner necks, more slope on the rump, and longer pasterns.

Today's Quarter Horses are used in many disciplines requiring strength, speed, and heart including ranch, pleasure riding, trail, cutting, reining, roping, polo, racing, team penning, and rodeo.

ROCKY MOUNTAIN HORSE

The Rocky Mountain Horse originated in Eastern Kentucky in the rugged Appalachian Mountains for use on the narrow trails that existed in the area before roads. Like the other gaited horses, Rocky Mountain Horses served all of the needs of a less well-to-do family living in these regions.

The Rocky Mountain Horse performs the typical smooth gaits and is built similarly to the other American gaited horses. The breed was informally created, with no written documentation, until the Rocky Mountain Horse Association incorporated in Kentucky in 1986 to establish guidelines. The first foundation sire in the late 1800s was a gaited colt with the chocolate-silver coloration. The second most famous stallion was Tobe who lived in the 1950s and passed along longevity to his many progeny as well as color, and the ambling, four beat lateral gait prized for its comfort.

Also known as the Rocky Mountain Pony, its characteristic color is a rare form of black called Chocolate Silver Dapple that produces a nearly white mane and tail contrasting with a body of dark or light chocolate brown enhanced with circular dapples.

The Rocky Mountain Horse stands between 14.2 and 15H.

AMERICAN SADDLEBRED

Saddlebred

The American Saddlebred does the walk, trot, and canter but also performs the slow gait and the rack. This is a pacing horse with lateral movement of both legs on the same side. The Saddlebred had been long touted as "The American Horse" since the late 1700s, and was once called "the Kentucky Saddler." Said to be the "oldest breed registry for an American horse breed," the American Saddle Horse Association was first created in 1891 then reorganized in 1980.

Originally, Thoroughbreds mixed with naturally gaited Hobby and Galloway horses from the British Isles created the Narragansett Pacer, a horse with the size and beauty of the Thoroughbred and the hardiness and smooth gaits of the smaller ponies. When crossed again to the Thoroughbred, the American Saddlebred emerged. The stallions Denmark FS and Harrison Chief 1606 are this breed's recognized foundation sires. When Arabian and Morgan blood was added, the horse became the high-stepping, elegant show horse it is today. The hooves of the Saddlebred are often grown long at the toes and artificially weighted to emphasize the horse's uphill carriage, but when trimmed naturally the horse can be used for pleasure and trail riding.

AMERICAN SHETLAND PONY

The American Shetland Pony was developed by mixing the Shetland Pony of Scotland with the Hackney Pony to create a more elegant, taller animal with higher leg action.

The American Shetland Pony Club was formed in 1888, and today includes The Classic American Shetland Pony, the Modern American Shetland Pony, the American Miniature Horse Registry, and the American Show Pony Registry. The Classic American Shetland Pony can stand up to 46". The Modern American Shetland has the same maximum height limit. Both are used as therapy animals, children's mounts, and agile perform-ance ponies for show harness, har-ness racing, and under saddle. The American Show Pony can measure up to 48" at the withers. Shetland ponies come in all colors.

American Shetland Pony

SPOTTED SADDLE HORSE

The Spotted Saddle Horse is a gaited horse with a beautiful pinto coloration as its hallmark. It possesses the same smooth, non-trotting ride of the other gaited breeds.

Formed in 1985, the Spotted Saddle Horse Breeders and Exhibitors Association set standards for their breed to include a sloping shoulder with a required 45 degree angle from withers to point of shoulder, long sloping hip, short back, and strong coupling. When viewed from the side, the Spotted Saddle Horse's bottomline (length along belly from leg to leg) is longer than its topline (length from neck to tail.) This is true for all gaited breeds because a longer bottom line allows for their exceptionally long stride. This breed can perform the show walk, the show gait, and the canter, as well as the rack, stepping pace, fox trot, and single foot. The show gait is unique to this breed, and is a faster version of the running walk, or show walk, which enables the horse to travel ten to 20 miles per hour.

Spotted Saddle Horses stand from 14.3 to 16H, and weigh from 900 to 1,100 pounds. They are exciting show horses to watch and ride.

A Spotted Saddle Horse must possess a white marking above its hocks (other than on the face), and must perform a smooth, easy, non-trotting gait to be eligible for registration.

STANDARDBRED

The Standardbred is the world's fastest harness-racing horse. Founded in America from Hambletonian, great grandson of Messenger, a British Thoroughbred, Standardbreds pull a sulky with a driver at the trot or pace, moving very rapidly for one mile.

Standardbreds are a relatively new breed, going back just over 200 years. The name was selected because the early trotters (pacers weren't popular until much later) were required to reach a standard speed for the mile in order to be registered. The first harness races occurred on roads and streets of major cities, which were often called Race Street. Pacers gained acceptance with the sport's first two-minute mile recorded in 1897 by Star Pointer. Dan Patch was one of the fastest and most popular Standardbred pacers, running the mile in 1:55. Niatross (son of Albatross, out of the mare Niagara Dream) ran the mile in 1:49 in 1970, and was the first harness horse to break 1:50.

Standardbreds are good-natured, friendly, easy learners with a calm disposition off the track. Standardbreds are often retrained, or trained off-track for pleasure, hunter-jumping, three-day eventing, cross-country, dressage, and as police and drill team mounts.

The foundation sire of the breed, Hambletonian, sired over 1,300 offspring between 1851 and 1875. Not quite as tall as the Thoroughbred at 15.2H, the Standardbred has a longer body, and appears mostly in bay, brown, and black. Standardbreds weigh only 800 to 1,000 pounds.

TENNESSEE WALKING HORSE

The Tennessee Walking Horse was created in Tennessee, of course, and the Tennessee Walking Horse Breeders and Exhibitors Association was incorporated there in 1935. Originally a combination of Standardbred, Thoroughbred, and Narragansett Pacer, the Tennessee Walking Horse exhibits the flat walk, running walk, and the rocking horse canter. It was bred for the use of southern plantation owners. In addition to the characteristic desirable head nod of American gaited horses, the Tennessee Walker's teeth are also said to click with each nod.

In addition to the normal method of shoeing horses, performance Tennessee Walkers were historically outfitted with high double- and triple-nailed padded shoes that elevated their hooves to accentuate their gaits for shows. The head and tail are elevated in these animated horses, and cadenced head nodding is a requirement.

Solid colors diluted from the champagne gene are found in this breed resulting in a glowing sheen to a light brown, light or dark gold, or ivory-colored coat. They have pinkish-brown skin and eyes of amber, green, or blue. As the old song "The Tennessee Stud" so aptly illustrates, *"The Tennessee Stud was long and lean, the color of sun, and his eyes were green."* Tennessee Walking Horses stand from 15 to 16H tall.

Tennessee Walker

There were three Gene Autry's Champion, but one that was used the most was a Tennessee Walking Horse.

HORSE BREEDS OF THE WORLD

Abyssinian

Akhal Teke

Albanian

Altai

American Cream Draft

American Creme and White

American Walking Pony

Andalusian

Andravida

Anglo-Kabarda

Appaloosa

Araappaloosa

Arabian

Ardennes

Argentine Criollo

Asturian

Australian Brumby

Australian Stock Horse

Azteca

Balearic

Baluchi

Banker

Ban-ei

Barb

Bashkir

Bashkir Curly

Basotho Pony

Belgian

Bhirum Pony

Bhotia Pony

Black Forest

Boer

Breton

Buckskin

Budyonny

Byelorussian Harness

Camargue

Campolina

Canadian

Carthusian

Caspian

Cayuse

Cheju

Chilean Corralero

Chincoteague Pony

Cleveland Bay

Clydesdale

Colorado Ranger Horse

Connemara Pony

Criollo (Uruguay)

Crioulo

Dales Pony

Danube

Dartmoor Pony

Deliboz

Djerma

Døle

Dongola

Dülmen Pony

Dutch Draft

Dutch Warmblood

East Bulgarian

Egyptian

Eriskay Pony

Estonian Native

Exmoor Pony

Faeroes Pony

Falabella

Fell Pony

Finnhorse

Fleuve

Florida Cracker

Fouta

Frederiksborg

French Saddlebred

French Trotter

Friesian

Galiceño

Galician Pony

Gelderlander

Gidran

Golden American Saddlebred

Gotland

Groningen

Guangxi

Hackney

Haflinger

Hanoverian

Hequ

Highland Pony

Hokkaido

Holsteiner

Hucul

Hungarian Warmblood

Icelandic

Iomud

Irish Draught

Jinzhou

Jutland

Kabarda

Karabair

Karabakh

Kazakh

Kerry Bog Pony

Kiger Mustang

Kirdi Pony

Kisber Felver

Kiso
Kladruby
Knabstrup
Kushum
Kustanai
Latvian
Lithuanian Heavy Draft
Lipizzan
Lokai
Losino
Lusitano
Malopolski
Mangalarga
Marwari
M'Bayar
Mérens Pony
Messara
Miniature
Misaki
Missouri Fox Trotting Horse
Miyako
Mongolian
Morab
Morgan
Moyle
Mustang
Murgese
National Show Horse
New Forest Pony
New Kirgiz
Newfoundland Pony

Noma
Nooitgedacht Pony
Noric
Nordland
Northeastern
North Swedish Horse
Norwegian Fjord
Ob
Oldenburg
Orlov Trotter
Paint
Palomino
Pantaneiro
Paso Fino
Percheron
Peruvian Paso
Pindos Pony
Pinia
Pintabian
Pinto
Polish Konik
Pony of the Americas
Pottok
Przewalski
Pyrenean Tarpan
Qatgani
Quarab
Quarter Horse
Quarter Pony
Racking Horse
Rocky Mountain Horse

Russian Don
Russian Heavy Draft
Russian Trotter
Saddlebred
Sanhe
Schleswiger Heavy Draft
Schwarzwälder Fuchs
Selle Francais
Shagya
Shetland Pony
Shire
Single-Footing Horse
Skyros Pony
Somali Pony
Sorraia
Soviet Heavy Draft
Spanish Mustang
Spanish-Barb
Spanish-Norman
Standardbred
Sudan Country-Bred
Suffolk
Swedish Warmblood
Taishuh
Tarpan
Tawleed
Tennessee Walking Horse
Tersk
Thessalian
Thoroughbred
Tokara

Tori
Trakehner
Ukrainian Saddle
Vlaamperd
Vladimir Heavy Draft
Vyatka
Welara Pony
Welsh Pony and Cob
West African Barb
Western Sudan Pony
Wielkopolski
Xilingol
Yakut
Yanqi
Yili
Yonaguni
Zaniskari Pony
Zhemaichu

Today's Horse

Over four million U.S. citizens participate in
recreational activities involving horses today,
with close to two million Americans owning horses.
Out of the seven million horses in the U.S. today, one
third are ridden out on the trail or in a backyard arena simply for the
fun of it. Millions of horse lovers who don't own any horses still sup-
port the plethora of horse fairs, magazines, expos, museums, books,
movies, and other products that involve these inspirational animals.

FLAT RACING

The development of the Thoroughbred racehorse in the seventeenth century was the start of today's modern racing. The important American races are the Kentucky Derby, the Preakness Stakes, the Belmont Stakes, and the Breeders' Cup. The Triple Crown consists of the first three races—there have been eleven Triple Crown winners, starting with Sir Barton in 1919, Gallant Fox (1930), Omaha (1935), War Admiral (1937), Whirlaway (1941), Count Fleet (1943), Assault (1946), Citation (1948), Secretariat (1973), Seattle Slew (1977), and Affirmed (1978). Races in the U.S. are run on "dirt" tracks, whereas races in Europe take place on prepared grass tracks. The English Derby is the most famous race in the world, and has been held annually since 1780.

Betting on horse races is a huge part of the industry. The highest amount won in one horse race is $3.6 million by Dubai Millennium in the Dubai World Cup in 2000. The greatest amount won in a year by a horse racing owner is $9,086,629 by Allen E. Paulson in 1996, and the highest horse racing career earnings by a filly is $8.3 million by Hokuto Vega from Japan.

Racing Thoroughbreds became popular sports in the 1800s in England. The first Kentucky Derby was run in 1875.

STEEPLECHASE

Steeplechasing began when two Irish foxhunters raced each other from one church to another (hence the name) in 1752. The modern sport is sort of a combination flat race with the addition of jumping obstacles commonly found while hunting from a horse (hedges, fences). In Europe, races are held both over natural country and over courses with very difficult manmade fences. The first steeplechase race in the United States was held in Washington DC in 1834.

The amateur sport of point-to-point racing is open to both men and women, and takes place in the UK and Ireland from February to late April each year. These races have a minimum distance of three miles with at least 18 fences.

Steeplechase trainers are based in the Eastern U.S., and concentrated mostly in Pennsylvania, Maryland, and Virginia.

The English Grand National is the most famous and demanding steeplechase in the world at over four miles long with 30 large fences. It has been run annually since 1839, except during World War II. Steeplechase horses run typically only six to ten times a year. All steeplechase horses are Thoroughbreds whose lineage must be proven.

HARNESS RACING

Chariot racing is the precursor to modern harness racing, and horses have raced in harness since at least 1300 BC. The U.S. is considered the world's leading harness-racing nation, where the sport is second only to Thoroughbred racing. Meadowlands in East Rutherford, New Jersey, is the leading racetrack in the U.S.

Pacing horses are preferred in the U.S.; they wear hobbles to prevent them from breaking their gait. The horses travel at speeds reaching 40 mph pulling a sulky. Trotting horses are preferred in Europe. Races occur for both trotters and pacers, but the two do not run races against each another.

Harness racing has its own Triple Crown, one each for trotters and pacers. The pacing races are the Cane Futurity at the Yonkers Racetrack in New York State, the Little Brown Jug in Delaware, Ohio, and the Messenger Stakes in Roosevelt. The trotting Triple Crown comprises the Hameltonian at Meadowlands, the Yonkers Trot in New York, and the Kentucky Futurity at Lexington's Red Mile Raceway.

Most harness racing horses wear sheepskin nosebands to limit their vision so they don't startle or shy at shadows.

DRESSAGE

Dressage comes from the French verb *dresser*, which means "teaching or schooling an animal." Dressage consists of precise, controlled moves (originally done for the battlefield and military parade grounds in Europe) performed in a specially sized and marked arena. The dressage arena must be 20 meters wide, and at least 40 meters long (a small dressage arena) or 60 meters long (a large arena). There is a deep, compacted solid base of soil underneath the footing of sand, which is ideally comprised of hard, angular, sharp quartz glacial or quarry sand that provides excellent traction. The sand must be screened to remove large pieces, and cleaned or washed to get rid of silt and clay. Since dressage tests require navigating, turning, and crossing the arena at designated intervals, there are cones or markers along the sides and ends of the arena to show riders the alphabetized points, "X" being the center of the arena where the dressage test begins and ends with a halt and salute to the judge.

Calmness, suppleness, concentration, and years of work on the part of both horse and rider are necessary for perfecting the roundest circles, straightest lines, sharpest turns, best leg-yield, shoulder-in, turns on the haunches, and extended trot. Advanced level moves include the canter pirouette, passage, piaffe, and flying lead changes. The Musical Kur, or Freestyle, so popular at the Olympics and at shows is a carefully choreographed dance of artistic expression between horse and rider. Ideally, the rider's cues to the horse should be nearly imperceptible. Any horse can be trained in dressage but at the higher levels the large, athletic warmbloods show the most expression and extension with their long necks and "bigger" movements.

The United States Dressage Federation, established in 1973, has nine regions with Chapters in all 50 states. Equestrian events of jumping and three-day eventing were included in the Olympics beginning in 1912, with dressage being added in 1928. Today Olympic Equestrian events are the only games where men and women compete in the same events, and both human and animal are declared medal winners.

For Dressage Federation recognized shows, competitors must wear white breeches, black or dark jacket, tall black boots, white shirt, and gloves. Advanced levels of competitors (from Prix St. Georges and up) must wear a black tailcoat, a yellow waist-coat, a black tophat, white breeches, white shirt, white gloves, spurs, and tall black boots. This type of serious, uniform attire is designed to put the focus almost entirely on the horse.

Show Jumping

Show jumping is an equine competitive sport in which horses are jumped over a course of fences, walls, and water-filled ditches or troughs. If a horse touches ("ticks") or knocks down the jump with his legs, a fault is added to the score. Hunter courses typically have eight jumps including natural logs, rails, gates, walls, and brush. Fences are set at a standard distance apart based on the 12-foot stride. Equitation courses test the skills of the rider, judging correct takeoff distance, accurate lines and turns, form and style. Refusals to jump as well as falls (of horse or rider or both) are faulted heavily.

Show Jumping has been enjoyed as an Olympic sport since 1912. The most suitable horses are the tall, powerful Thoroughbreds and the warmblooded breeds, but many breeds participate in jumping, including ponies.

Jump saddles have a more slanted leg flap for the leg position required to keep the person's seat elevated with inside of knees in close contact during jumps. There are no horns or large skirts on English saddles. They are lightweight, small, and round on all edges. Stirrups are metal, and stirrup leathers are made of a thin belt of leather. Saddle pads are thin and usually white for shows.

THREE-DAY EVENTING

A dressage test, a round of stadium jumping, and then a difficult cross-country course face the same horse and rider in three consecutive days in this sport. The first day is a set of 20 dressage moves to gauge horse and rider communication and partnership, followed on the second day by two "road and track" (both long and short races),

which cover flat ground in a set time at a fast trot or canter, a steeplechase over brush jumps, and a cross-country jump over up to 35 obstacles including high jumps, water, and ditches. The third day consists of stadium jumping over 10 to 12 obstacles. There is a vet check the second day before the strenuous cross country phase, and any horse that does not pass is eliminated. Every year the Rolex Kentucky Three-Day Event is held at the Kentucky Horse Park with world class competitors.

The three-day event was first called "The Military" and consisted of a 33-mile long-distance ride, a 2-mile steeplechase, show jumping, and then a dressage test. Active-duty officers on military horses competed in the 1912 Olympics.

DRIVING

In-hand horse driving from the small one-person exercise carts to the large carriages or wagons has become a popular recreational outlet. Successful pleasure driving includes obstacle negotiating, obedient adherence to commands and cues, and a solid halt until a command to walk on is given. Any breed or size adult horse or pony can be taught to drive as long as they are properly desensitized to the harness, cart, traffic, and road conditions, and well-trained in the cues and commands. It is very important to choose a strong harness that fits each individual animal with all the necessary parts like a breast collar, breeching, and padding for optimal safety and comfort.

There are international driving competitions for teams of four horses (four-in-hand teams), pairs, tandems, and some single horse and pony events.

Scurry Driving involves pony pairs running a mini-obstacle course in the shortest time. There are two height divisions, 48" and under and 48" to 56". Fast, agile ponies are the best for this sport.

HORSE SHOWS

Horse Shows help young and old riders alike gauge their abilities and take pride in their equestrian accomplishments. There are many sanctioned horse shows in all equine disciplines occurring year round all over the world. The National Horse Show in Madison Square Garden in New York City was begun in 1883 (with international show jumping competition added in 1911). Over a quarter of a million children participate in 4-H and Pony Club shows in the U.S. Typical classes in horse shows are Western and English Pleasure and Equitation, Showmanship at Halter, Trail, Hunter and Jumper, and Gymkhana.

RODEO

The first official rodeo was held on July 4, 1886, in Prescott, Arizona, say some accounts. At the turn of the century, rodeos were combined with the "Wild West" show, and included wagon races, bull-riding, and steer wrestling. The Professional Rodeo Cowboy's Association (PRCA) cites Deer Trail, Colorado, in 1864 as the location of the first rodeo competition, when cowboys from local ranches met to decide who was best at performing their daily ranch chores of roping and riding a bucking animal. Rodeo is said to be the only sport derived from an industry, although today's pro rodeo competitors earn quite a bit more money, and travel the PRCA circuit up to 200 days a year in custom-made rigs or by private airplane. Today more than 800 paid attendance rodeos are held annually. The Pro Rodeo Hall of Fame and Museum of the American Cowboy are in Colorado Springs, Colorado.

Modern Rodeo events include calf roping, steer roping, steer wrestling, bareback bronc riding, saddle bronc riding, and bull riding. The clowns who protect the bull riders are always crowd favorites as well as daring performers and superb athletes. In addition to human champions, superior bulls and horses are also honored with yearly

"Amazing! The kid's a natural. I've never seen anyone stick to a saddle quite like that!"

© Leigh Rubin

awards. The American Quarter Horse is the traditional mount of rodeo events.

In 1948 three ranch women organized an all-girl rodeo in Amarillo, Texas, which was the first of its kind. Cowgirls from Texas and neighboring states came together to compete in calf roping, team roping, bull and bronc riding, barrel racing, and other events. At this event the Girls Rodeo Association (GRA) was born. In 1979, the organization had almost 2,000 members and held 15 sanctioned all-girl shows. In 1981 it changed its name to the Women's Professional Rodeo Association. Many of its barrel racers also compete in PRCA barrel events as well.

COWGIRLS

Much has been written about cowboys and generals, but The Cowgirl Hall of Fame opened in 1975 in Ft. Worth, Texas, and is the only museum in the world honoring the lives of legendary women who embodied the pioneer spirit of the American West. 172 women have been inducted into the Cowgirl Hall of Fame, including Bertha Blancett, the first woman to ride broncs at Cheyenne and a Wild West show bronc rider; Faye Blackstone, who created new trick riding stunts including the Reverse Fender Drag; Texas Rose Bascom, the "Queen of the Trick Ropers"; Anna Lee Aldred, the first woman jockey in the U.S.; Mary Jo Milner, a cutting horse breeder with an unprecedented six National Cutting Horse Association Non-Pro World Championships; and Lindy Burch, the first female NCHA Open World Champion, and first female president of the NCHA.

TRAIL RIDING

In addition to just getting on your horse and going for a trek into the wood, hills, fields, across the streams, and through the forests near your home or barn, there are many highly organized trail rides held all over the U.S. Usually involving an overnight campout, these social events for man and horse often include a big dinner, dance, happy hour, and much merriment. Annual participants get together and reminisce after the usually long, challenging trail ride is over.

"Trail Trials" is a judged obstacle competition that is not a timed race, but completion of each obstacle (usually up to 15) with as few penalties as possible is the goal. Including an overnight campout, there are awards and meals. Obstacles are often highly creative, but are supposed to be limited to what might be found on a trail including pack llamas, donkeys, dogs, old vehicles, and all sorts of natural hazards and oddities.

Trail classes are regularly held at horse shows and involve the successful negotiation and adherence to a pattern of completion over poles, through gates, and around obstacles at different rates of speed and direction. Overnight trail rides into scenic areas are common, as are organized trail rides through Africa, Ireland, South America, New Zealand and other scenic countries.

ENDURANCE AND DISTANCE RIDING

Long distance endurance rides are races of 50 to 100 miles per day where the same horse and rider cover a course within a specified maximum time (12 hours for the 50-miler and 24 hours for the 100-miler). Limited Distance rides between 25 and 35 miles per day are mainly for novices. The focus of endurance is proper nutrition, concentration, and conditioning of both horse and rider. This requires miles of practice every day to build stamina in the horse. Courses include horse camping. Token awards are given to everyone who finishes, but the highest go to the fastest finisher, the winners of each weight division (weight of rider and tack), and the best conditioned

horse (deemed by veterinarians who check pulse, temperature, and soundness at the trot at numerous checkpoints). Arabian horses predominate in this sport, but it is open to any type or breed of horse or mule that is at least five years old. The American Endurance Ride Conference (AERC) has a great handbook, and other pertinent information available on this sport on their website.

HUNTING

American fox hunters do not set out to kill their quarry as they did in England, and because of a lack of foxes, they often hunt coyotes. In the U.S., a successful fox hunt ends when the fox enters its den in the ground. Then the hounds are praised for their tenacity, and the fox (or wily coyote) lives to run another day. American fox hunters brag that they haven't actually caught the fox for years, and as a result there has been a lot less organized opposition to fox hunting in the U.S. Fox hunt enthusiasts enjoy the rural chase and gallop across the scenic countryside, and the fence jumping. More than 150 fox hunts occur in the U.S. each year. The most suitable horses for fox hunting are Thoroughbreds and the warmblood breeds.

France has the oldest tradition of hunting with horses and hounds, and in Britain, these hunts have been taking place since the eleventh century.

POLO

The British first noticed polo being played in Persia on tiny, 12-hand ponies, and adopted the sport. (The word polo comes from the Tibetan "pulu," meaning ball.) Polo "ponies" have been documented in England since 1893, even though today's polo mounts are of standard horse size, around 15 hands. Polo is played on a ten-acre grassy field (the size of ten football fields) with goal posts at each end set eight yards apart. Polo players move a small plastic ball down the field with bamboo mallets that have hardwood heads while jostling and bumping each other and racing at top speed. Shots can be made off all sides of the horse, from under the neck, across the tail, or the difficult under the belly shot. Polo horses in the U.S. are primarily Thoroughbreds (often with race track experience) and 90 percent or more are mares. Other breeds notable for polo are the Argentine Criollo crossed with Thoroughbreds, and the Thoroughbred Quarter Horse mixes.

VAULTING

Since Roman times vaulting on horseback has been an acrobatic sport and a method of teaching children to ride. In Medieval days vaulting was used to train knights. In 1956, a woman brought back a 16mm film of vaulting from Europe, and introduced it to her Pony Club members in California. In 1966, The American Vaulting Association was founded. Vaulting utilizes a large, calm, methodically-gaited horse wearing a vaulting saddle and two leather loops (called Cossack straps) for the vaulter's feet. The horse travels in a 20 meter circle on a longe line in an arena with soft footing. Vaulters practice their vault-off, and compulsory and freestyle moves on a vaulting barrel prior to working on horseback. In competition a team has eight members and each performs six basic exercises. At the advanced level, a group of three riders may perform on the same horse all together.

One trick pony

CIVIL WAR REENACTMENTS

The National Civil War Association educates the public about the people and events of the Civil War with military and civilian encampments and staged battles. Volunteers dress in period clothing, and own their own historic equipment and weapons. Horses play a prominent role in these displays, and school programs show kids and other visitors what life was like back in the nineteenth century.

"Stop it! Stop this horseplay immediately."

Draft Horse Pulling

Draft Horse Pulling consists of a team of horses hitched to a heavy load. The team that can move the heaviest load in eight seconds is the winner. A good pulling horse can cost up to $20,000, and there are an estimated 200 pulling teams in the state of Michigan alone. There are Draft Horse shows dedicated solely to these gentle giants of the horse world nationwide in which large monetary prizes for performance and halter divisions are awarded.

WESTERN RIDING ATTIRE AND TACK

Western show outfits depend somewhat on
the class entered. Western Pleasure,
Horsemanship/Equitation, and Trail require chaps
over starched jeans or show pants, a tunic top or
blouse or stretchy shirt with or without a vest,
jackets, blazers, a western hat, western boots, belt
and buckle. The color of the shirt and outfit should
coordinate with the horse's color, and their saddle
blanket. Men's attire includes a tie or scarf in a

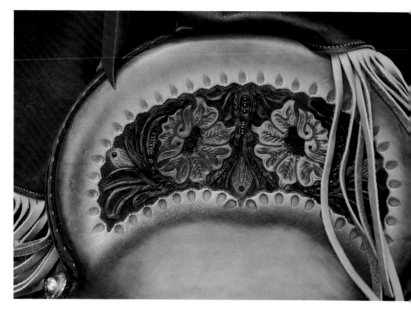

square knot. In Showmanship, Halter, Reining, and Cutting the attire
can be more casual yet always complimenting the horse and tack.

    Western saddles come in show and trail styles, leather and syn-
thetic, brown or black usually tooled with designs. They weigh from
20 pounds on up—40 is an average weight—with a girth, a back
cinch, leather stirrups, and a leather skirting that is either square or
round. Stirrup leathers for adjusting length of stirrups are underneath
the leg flaps. Most Western saddles have horns which were originally
used to dally a rope around, but today are mostly for looks. It is not
considered proper form to hold onto the saddle horn for comfort or
balance during a ride, except maybe in an emergency.

HORSE THOUGHTS

The U.S. has recently seen a significant increase in first-time horse buyers, as well as riders over the age of 50, in the past ten years. Clinics, training methods, horse acupuncture, acupressure, massage, dentistry, herbal treatments, trimming your own horse, and all manner of interesting equine specialties abound today.

"Backyard breeders" owning a few mares, inseminating mares, or taking them to someone else's stallion to be bred, and raising and selling the foals are becoming more prevalent.

The barn business is booming, tack stores, feed dealers, and new accessories for the horse increase daily. Could fast-paced, technologically-ruled America actually be going backwards, riding into a saner quieter, simpler, centered, and more balanced state of mind? Horse people certainly hope so!

Photo Credits

Page 2 © J-J Alcalay/Peter Arnold, Inc.

Page 5 © Bob Langrish

Page 6 © M. Watson/Ardea London

Page 7 © François Gohier/Ardea London

Page 8 © Bob Langrish

Page 9 © Tom & Pat Leeson/Ardea London

Page 10 © Adrian Warren/Ardea London

Page 13 © Bob Langrish

Page 14 © Londie G. Padelsky

Page 15 © Bob Langrish

Page 17 © Chris Knights/Ardea London

Page 21 © Terry Wild Studio, Inc.

Page 24 © Bob Langrish

Page 25 © wyomingtailsandtrails.com

Page 26 © Master Sgt. Jim Varhegyi

Page 28 © Robert Maier/AnimalsAnimals

Page 29 Gemma Giannini/Grant Heilman
   Photography, Inc.

Page 30 © Bob Langrish

Page 31 © Liz & Tony Bomford/Ardea London

Page 32 © Dusty L. Perin

Page 33 © Tom & Pat Leeson

Page 34 © Bob Langrish

Page 35 © Bob Langrish

Page 36 © Bob Langrish

Page 37 © Bob Langrish

Page 38 © Bob Langrish

Page 39 © Sabine Stuewer

Page 40 © Ron Kimball

Page 41 © Ron Kimball

Page 42 © Bob Langrish

Page 43 © Ron Kimball

Page 44 © Dusty L. Perin

Page 45 © Bob Langrish

Page 46 © Dusty L. Perin

Page 47 © Dusty L. Perin

Page 48 © Robert Maier/AnimalsAnimals

Page 49 © Robert Maier/AnimalsAnimals

Page 50 © Bob Langrish

Page 51 © Dusty L. Perin

Page 52 (top) © Bob Langrish; (bottom) © Robert
   Maier/AnimalsAnimals

Page 53 © Sabine Stuewer

Page 54 © Sabine Stuewer

Page 55 © Bob Langrish

Page 56 © Dusty L. Perin

Page 57 © Ardea London

Page 58 © Bob Langrish

Page 59 © Bob Langrish

Page 61 © Bob Langrish

Page 62 © David Dixon/Ardea London

Page 63 © Dusty L. Perin

Page 64 © Bob Langrish

Page 65 © Sabine Stuewer

Page 66 © John Daniels/Ardea London

Page 67 © John Daniels/Ardea London

Page 68 © Bob Langrish

Page 69 © Bob Langrish

Page 70 © Yva Momatiuk-John Eastcott/Minden
   Pictures

Page 71 © Londie G. Padelsky

Page 72 © Bob Langrish

Page 73 © Jean-Paul Ferrero/Ardea London

Page 74 © Bob Langrish

Page 75 © Dusty L. Perin

Page 76 © Bob Langrish

Page 77 © Dusty L. Perin

Page 78 © Bob Langrish

Page 79 © Dusty L. Perin

Page 80 © John Daniels/Ardea London

Page 81 © Bob Langrish

Page 82 © Bob Langrish

Page 83 © Denver Bryan/www.DenverBryan.com

Page 84 © Bob Langrish

Page 85 © Bob Langrish

Page 86 © Bob Langrish

Page 87 © Bob Langrish

Page 88 © Bob Langrish

Page 89 © Bob Langrish

Page 90 © Dusty L. Perin

Page 91 © Bob Langrish

Page 92 © Bob Langrish

Page 93 © Jean-Paul Ferrero/Ardea London

Page 94 © Bob Langrish

Page 95 © Sabine Stuewer

Page 96 © Bob Langrish

Page 97 © Bob Langrish

Page 98 © Bob Langrish

Page 99 © Bob Langrish

Page 100 © Bob Langrish

Page 101 © Bob Langrish

Page 102 © Bob Langrish

Page 103 © Bob Langrish

Page 104 © Bob Langrish

Page 105 © Bob Langrish

Page 106 © Bob Langrish

Page 107 © Londie G. Padelsky

Page 108 © Londie G. Padelsky

Page 109 (top) © Dusty L. Perin; (bottom) © Bob
   Langrish

Page 112 © Bob Langrish

Page 113 © Dusty L. Perin

Page 114 © Dusty L. Perin

Page 115 (top & bottom) © Londie G. Padelsky

Page 116 © Bob Langrish

Page 117 © Bob Langrish

Page 120 © Jean-Paul Ferrego/Ardea London